# BASKETBALL'S FASTEST HANDS

LOU SAHADI

SCHOLASTIC BOOK SERVICES
New York Toronto London Auckland Sydney Tokyo

Photos: pp. 11, 67—Focus on Sports; p. 89—Jim Walker/Norfolk Virginian Pilot

No part of this publication may be reproduced in whole or in part, or stored in a retrieval system, or transmitted in any form or by any means, electronic, mechanical, photocopying, recording, or otherwise, without written permission of the publisher. For information regarding permission, write to Scholastic Book Services, 50 West 44th Street, New York, NY 10036.

Copyright © 1977 by Lou Sahadi. All rights reserved. Published by Scholastic Book Services, a division of Scholastic Magazines, Inc.

12 11 10 9 8 7 6 5 4 3 2 1    1    7 8 9/7 0 1 2/8

Printed in the U.S.A.    06

# Contents

Vital Ingredient ......................... 1
Slick Watts: Ball Thief .................. 5
Tiny Archibald: Magic Dribbler ........... 17
Dave Bing: The Come-Back Kid .......... 29
Jo Jo White: The Take-Charge Guy ....... 39
Gail Goodrich: He Does It All ............ 51
Calvin Murphy: Mighty Mite With Clout ... 60
Norm Van Lier: Thinking Big ............ 71
Mack Calvin: Up From the ABA .......... 83

# Vital Ingredient

Imagine a basketball team made up of five starters who stand 7-feet, 6-10, 6-9, 6-9, and 6-8. Dynamite! A dream team! Right? Unbeatable! Right?

Wrong.

Something very important would be missing in this "unbeatable" bunch—two smaller backcourt men who have the vital skills to make things happen. If anyone thinks the little guy doesn't have a place in professional basketball, he's badly mistaken.

For a moment, just think about a game between two teams of giants. The game would probably be nothing more than constant firing the ball toward the hoop from in close, or off the backboard, and lots of leaping for rebounds.

It wouldn't make for very exciting basketball. That's where the little guys come in. They're as necessary to today's game as the ball itself. It's the little guys with the lightning reflexes and fast hands who make things happen on the basketball floor—and in so many ways that they're genuine heroes to thousands of fans.

For example take dribbling. What is more exciting than seeing a short guard dribbling in and around the taller players. Notice the look of frustration from the taller opponent as the big man attempts to knock the ball away. Rarely does he succeed. More often he will foul the dribbler. Yet all the while the dribbler is penetrating the defense. Often his tactics will shake a teammate loose for an easy basket. Or he can drive with the ball for an easy lay-up. In any case, he is making things happen.

Take a fast break, for instance—one of the most exciting maneuvers in basketball. It's true it begins with a defensive rebound from one of the big forwards or the center. But it's the little guy that makes it work. He'll quickly dribble the ball upcourt and penetrate as deep as he can in the attack zone before passing off to a fast-breaking teammate on either side of the lane.

Now take passing. Who better than a guard can fire a more accurate pass? That is one of the skills he has to master. He realizes that a good pass is expected of him, either in setting up a planned play or in being ready to complete a free-lance play. In either situation, he has to deliver a quick, accurate pass either in the air or bouncing it at the right moment.

That's one good reason why the little guys are

credited with so many assists when a basket is made. While the end result is a field goal, it is a pass delivered on time that accounts for the score. It's simple. The forwards and center are expected to score most of the points. But by the same token, the guards are expected to get the ball to them.

And if they don't, it's mostly because the pass is broken up. And by whom? By a defensive guard, of course. Because of his size, a guard has to be quick. He has to have fast hands. He has to be quick enough to anticipate the pass and quick enough to stop it. A lot of times he is so quick, he can steal the ball out of his opponent's hands. That's how fast his reflexes are. Often the quick steal results in an easy basket, which in some cases demoralizes the opposing team.

It is not that a guard looks for the easy bucket all the time. Instead, he works hard for his basket. And since he usually has to score his basket from outside, he must be an accurate shooter. There is no prettier sight in basketball than a guard firing a one-hand jump shot that splits the cords with a snap. The sound of the ball making contact with the net is enough to generate excitement in an arena.

In a close game, when the trailing team needs to get the ball and score a basket, a coach will often pull out one of his tall forwards and put in a small guard. It enables him to have three guards on the floor at the same time. He wants the guards to harrass the opposing team, either by stealing the ball or putting on so much pressure that the other team will turn over the ball.

So, the little guards are very important to a pro basketball team. They are needed offensively and defensively. Size is really not that important, as long as they are quick and agile, are good shooters, and have a good knowledge of what the game of basketball is all about. They are the playmakers, the guys that make things happen. Most often they are the crowd pleasers, generating cheers for their exciting play.

As is the case of Jo Jo White, the veteran guard of the Boston Celtics. His exciting play, shooting, passing, directing the Celtics' attack earned him the Most Valuable Player award of the 1975-76 championship series against the Phoenix Suns. White was the trigger of the Boston offense, scoring 130 points in six games. His remarkable all-around effort in the fifth game of the series turned the tide in Boston's favor.

White is one of the many star guards in the National Basketball Association. The Celtics couldn't have won the NBA championship without him. There are a number of others like him. In pro basketball, players 6-3 and under are considered small men. But they have the fastest hands in basketball. And the game is so much better for it....

# SLICK WATTS
## Ball Thief

Nobody thought much of Don "Slick" Watts. In the 1973 National Basketball Association college player draft, nobody picked him. True, he was only 6-1, was from the small town of Rolling Fork, Mississippi, and he played for a little school, Xavier University of New Orleans; and the professional scouts didn't think much of his chances. At best, they felt he was just a good college player. Nothing more. But they didn't know one important thing: just how much determination Watts had.

His college coach, Bob Hopkins, a former pro player himself, knew. He honestly felt that Watts could play pro ball. He knew the type of person Watts was and the kind of desire and attitude he had. So, Hopkins decided to stick his neck out. He called Bill Russell, the coach of the Seattle SuperSonics, to convince him of Watts' ability to make it in the pros. Russell also happened to be

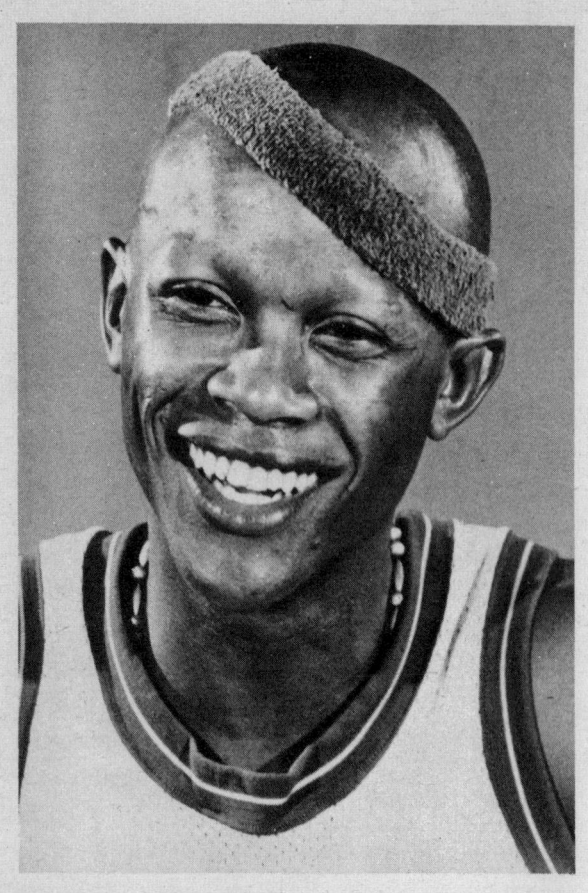

Slick Watts: noted for his shaven skull and sweat band.

Hopkins' cousin and it was easy for him to agree to take a look at Watts.

But first Russell wanted to talk to Watts on the phone. "Man, can you play?" asked Russell.

"Yes, sir, I can play," answered Watts without hesitating.

"You know you're very little and you'll have to prove an awful lot of things," warned Russell.

"Yes, sir, I can play," repeated Watts.

Before talking to Russell, Watts had been depressed. He had his heart set on playing pro ball and he waited anxiously for some team to draft him. But Russell's phone call changed all that.

"I hadn't been drafted by anybody through all 10 rounds," he remembered. "I was really down and ready to give up hopes of playing ball and just become a school teacher. Then Hopkins came through and got me a chance to try out with the Sonics.

"I got all fired up when Russell sent me a plane ticket from New Orleans to Seattle. The same week I sold all my furniture and told all my friends that I wasn't coming back. They all shook their heads. They said I'd be back—that I was too small. But I was determined to play pro ball."

Hopkins accompanied Watts to Seattle. He wanted to give the youngster confidence. Besides, he knew how tough the pro tryout camps were. And he also knew that Russell wouldn't offer Watts any encouragement.

"The first thing Russell said to me was that if I couldn't run I'd be at the unemployment office pretty quickly," said Watts.

The first few days of practice, Watts didn't get a chance to play much. He began to feel he was only there because Russell did his cousin a favor. But Russell wasn't rushing Watts. When he did give the youngster his chance, Watts made the most of it. He showed quickness and he hustled, and the sportswriters were so impressed they began writing about a little bald-headed player taking the ball away from everybody.

The more he played, the more impressive he was. But he didn't hear any words of encouragement from Russell. That's Russell's way. He doesn't talk much to begin with and he doesn't get overly excited about rookies anyway. On the last day of the tryouts, Watts learned about his chances. Until then, Russell only admitted that the little guy was the fastest man he'd ever seen on a court and nicknamed him "Slick."

"Russell called us into the locker room to tell us who was going to get invited back to veterans camp," said Watts. "Everybody looked down at the floor and it was quiet. 'Harold Fox!' shouted Russell. Then he named another rookie from South Carolina—I can't remember his name—and then Russell finished by shouting, 'Slick Watts.'

"Boy, was I excited! Later I called my father in

New Orleans. One test was passed, and eight days to go. 'Daddy,' I told him, 'keep prayin' for your boy. They gave me a contract to sign but it wasn't for any money. It just said that if I got hurt in veterans camp I couldn't sue the Sonics.' "

The first day of camp, Russell really worked them, trying to see who had heart. "Man, all them cats nearly died the way he worked us. I had a bad back, a slipped disc. I used to carry a pillow to class at Xavier to keep it from hurting when I sat in a chair. It was just killing me in camp and one day Russell walked over and says, 'Kid, can't you touch your toes?'

"I'd had to pay a little boy to put my socks on that day, my back was hurting so bad. But I just reached down to that floor. Pain shot up my legs and across my back. My hands were shaking, but I did it. Russell just grinned at me. I could have paralyzed myself, but I had to do it."

Training camp was rough and Russell was giving Watts a severe test. He wanted to see how much heart the little rookie had, how badly he wanted to play pro ball. Day after day Watts finished practice so tired that all he did was to fall into bed. He almost gave up. He called his father one night and told him it wasn't worth it. But his father told him to stick it out, that he could make it.

Watts figured that training camp would be tough but he never realized just how rough it would be. The phone call to his father gave him new strength. He turned up at practice the next day raring to go.

He really hustled during a scrimmage. He dove for loose balls, stole balls out of the veterans' hands, and was a bundle of energy in scoring baskets. He was truly making some of the veterans look bad. And Russell made a point of it, too, by stopping the action.

"Who's checking you, kid?" asked Russell.

"Nobody, sir," Watts shouted back.

By the time the first week ended, Russell had seen enough. He knew that Watts had the talent to play in the NBA. He gave Watts a contract for $23,000 with a $1500 bonus.

"He said, 'Sign here, son. You're a pro player.' He gave me the $1500 for signing. I came back the next day and asked for more. I was the only rookie to make the club. I sure had nerve for asking.

"Russell said, 'But you're just a free agent.'

" 'But, I can play, sir,' I said. So he gave me another $1,000 and I sent the money home to my mother and father.

"Then, one day during the exhibition season, Russell called me over and I went for a ride in his car.

"He said, 'Kid, you're going to be all right. In four years you'll be ready.' I said to myself, 'Four years? No, man, you just don't know.' "

Watts escapes his man and goes up for the two-pointer.

Russell knew he had a ball player. He also knew it would take a little time for Watts to develop as a pro. He knew that Watts had quick hands and would hustle. He also felt that in time Watts would develop into one of the NBA's star guards.

Russell didn't rush Watts. In his rookie season, Watts played in only 62 games. But in his second year in 1974-75, Watts played in every game and started to gain some notice around the league by playing well in the playoffs. He also established himself as a starter and became a favorite among the Seattle fans.

He really captured their hearts in a game against the Portland Trail Blazers. It was the most talked about game of the season and one of the most exciting victories in Seattle's history.

With two minutes remaining in the third quarter, the Sonics were trailing the Trail Blazers by 24 points. But Watts, hustling all over the floor, led a spirited Sonics' rally. Finally, with only 1:29 left in the game, they caught Portland at 102-102.

In a jump-ball situation moments later, Portland appeared to have the edge as center Bill Walton was matched against the Sonics' John Brister. However, Watts sized up the situation. He perfectly anticipated where the taller Walton would tap the ball. When the play began, he streaked between Larry Steele and Geoff Petrie of the Trail Blazers and cleverly stole the ball.

The theft led to the deciding basket as the SuperSonics won.

"Anticipation is the name of the game for a little backcourt man in the pro's," says Watts. Actually, he could have added college, high school, or bantam league play. The little man must take advantage not only of his quickness and his fast hands but he should also develop a sense of where and how the action flows. Watts is a master at anticipating the foe's moves and knows when to drop off his own man and make an effort to block or even steal a pass to another player. "I watch their eyes," he says. "I even try to read their wrists as they prepare to pass the ball."

Yet, he has to be so quick that he can scramble back onto his own man, and not let him loose for a quick cut to the basket.

"For me," says Watts, "there's as much satisfaction in stealing the ball as there is in making an assist for a basket. If you keep stealing that ball from the other guys, you make such a pest of yourself that it can throw their whole game off balance."

As a starter in the playoffs that year, he averaged 11 points and seven assists in the nine games the Sonics played. In the final game of the Western Division semi-finals, which Seattle lost to the champion Golden State Warriors, Watts played the entire 48 minutes. He scored 24 points, had 11 assists and four steals. Russell called it one of the greatest performances he'd ever seen from a small backcourt man. Sportswriters agreed that Watts was now entitled to his nickname of "Slick."

"Slick's a good player, a great one for us," praised Russell. "I said at the beginning that the one thing that could help us more than his improvement as a player would be for his enthusiasm to become contagious. And it has. The chemistry on this team is excellent, like the old Celtics. And Slick is the guy who does the most to keep it that way."

Watts also makes Sonic fans happy. Watts has made over 500 appearances around Seattle. He is in demand everywhere. He never refuses a requested appearance unless his schedule is filled. Watts visits hospitals, elementary schools, and high schools. In an elementary school he will bend down and let the little kids rub his shiny head. His answers to the children's questions delight both the youngsters and teachers. They are captivated with the headband he wears to "keep the hair out of his eyes." He shaves his head and oils it, "so I can slip through the other team's defense easier." He never refuses an autograph except just before a game. Fans wait for him from the time he parks his car and then follow him all the way to the dressing room, which sometimes throws off his shooting. He solved that problem by signing a few hundred index cards ahead of time and now hands them out on the way into the arena. And, after a game, he signs until the last fan is gone.

"Giving pleasure is the greatest thing a person can do in his life," explained Watts. "I tell them 'thank you' for treating me the way you'd treat a superstar. But you know something—I saw my first pro basketball player when I got on the court to play against him. I want the kids to know that I'm just like them, that I'm no superman just because I play ball. I am part of this community and it is a beautiful place. God picked it out just for me and said, 'Slick, I got this little heaven for you. I call it Seattle.' If they ever trade me, I'll retire."

The Sonics' assistant general manager, Bob Walsh, says he's never met a person with the magnetism of Slick Watts.

"He's mystical," exclaims Walsh. "He's the kind of guy who can make you believe anything he says."

He certainly made Russell and the rest of the front office believers by his actions on the court. Before the 1975-76 season began, the Sonics traded All-Pro guard Archie Clark to the Detroit Pistons, which made Watts a starter and a $100,000 player. He was earning $45,000 but got a new contract with a special clause unknown before in sports circles. If the Sonics felt that Watts' play didn't merit the raise, they could refuse to pay part of his salary.

So what did Watts do? He went out and enjoyed the best year of his career. He became the first player to win the assists average title and steals championship in the same season. Watts averaged 8.1 assists a game and stole 261 passes in 82 games for an average of 3.1 per contest. He also averaged 13 points a game.

"I'm not asked to be a scorer and I do believe it takes more guts and an unselfish attitude to go for assists rather than scoring," said Watts.

Is it any wonder Sonic fans love Watts?

# TINY ARCHIBALD
## Magic Dribbler

The ghetto is always there. But that's the way Nate Archibald wants it. While most ghetto kids would like to forget it, Archibald does not. Fact is, the ghetto is still a way of life to him. And every summer, the lightning-quick six-foot guard of the New York Nets returns to the South Bronx in New York to help black kids find a better way of life. He gives them hope—hope that one day they, too, can leave the ghetto like Archibald did.

What Archibald does for the kids is something out of the ordinary. Far above it. He not only helped form the Harlem Professional Basketball League, but he plays in it several times a week. On a couple of other nights during the week, he is busy coaching one of his two teams in a youth league he developed with assistance from a sporting goods manufacturer. And on any given afternoon, Archibald hangs around the playground

**Nate Archibald: KC Kings star comes home to New York.**

shooting baskets and giving kids pointers on the game he loves so much.

He does all this because he is a low-keyed superstar. He does so unselfishly because he is not a person who is awed by flashy clothes and night life. He even did so by leaving his wife and four children home in Kansas City, before being traded to the Nets, because his wife understood Nate's deep-down dedication to help unfortunate youngsters. Archibald is a product of the ghetto and he knows the only way out for other kids is to help.

So every summer, for the past six years, Archibald has returned to the garbage-littered streets of the Bronx where crime and violence are still a way of life. Up until two years ago he and his family lived with his mother and brothers and sisters until he bought them a house and a better way of life on Long Island. It was a promise he made to his mother. His family's welfare has always been important to him.

"He said he was going to buy me a home and he did," said his mother, Mrs. Julia Archibald. "He's always stuck in there when the going was rough. Nate was 14 years old when his father left home. But Nate helped out with his five brothers and sisters as much as possible and he still helps the family."

It would have been so easy for Archibald to have gone the way of many ghetto kids. The temptation of drugs, crime, and gang wars was all around him when he was growing up. The fact that he was so small didn't help him either. Most of the time the bigger kids wouldn't let Nate play with them. So Nate would shoot baskets by himself and go one-on-one with anyone he could find, to develop his skills.

Still, Archibald never really had the deep desire to play professional basketball. Most kids his age would dream about it, but Nate felt he would never be big enough. He liked playing basketball because it was the best way to pass away the time and keep out of trouble.

When he entered high school, Archibald had developed into an excellent player for a kid his size. He was quick and he could dribble skillfully. He looked forward to playing on the school team his sophomore year. However, he didn't make the team and he became discouraged. He tried again his junior year but lost any chance he had of making the team when, again discouraged, he walked off the floor during a practice session.

Floyd Lane, who coached at a community college, took Archibald under his wing. Lane explained that basketball was one way to further his education as a means of getting out of the ghetto. Lane then met with Archibald's high school coach and talked him into giving Archibald another chance. The "chance" turned into All-City honors in his senior year.

Despite his size, Archibald impressed a

number of college scouts. However, getting into college was a problem.

"It wasn't until then that I realized how important grades were," admitted Archibald. "I wasn't dumb or anything, but I didn't study and my grades weren't up to par to get me into a four-year college. I finally obtained a scholarship to Arizona Junior College. I played fairly good ball there and pushed my academic average up around a B level. After Arizona, I got a two-year scholarship to the University of Texas at El Paso.

"That's what I try to tell the kids in the ghetto—make an effort in the classroom FIRST! The thing around the community now is to become a professional athlete. But the message I try to give them is that not everyone can be one. A lot of guys don't make it, and simply say, 'Forget it. If I can't play ball, I don't want to do nothing.' I tell the kids, 'Go to school to play ball AND get an education. Prepare yourself for the rest of your life.'"

Although he didn't make any All-America teams, Archibald played well his final two years of college. He averaged 16 points a game and led the team in assists. Still, he felt his chances of playing pro ball weren't very good. Archibald personally, and the school in general, didn't receive much publicity. However, the then Cincinnati Royals had their eye on Archibald and made him their number-two draft pick in 1970.

In his first pro season, Archibald didn't let the Royals down. Although he was considered too small by many, Archibald proved that a good little man can make it. He averaged 16 points and 9.6 assists a game. He displayed confidence right from the start.

"Archibald took over from the time he set foot into our camp," said Cincinnati coach Bob Cousy, an all-time NBA great who had played with the Boston Celtics. "For a little guy, he had great determination and spunk. He wasn't afraid to take on any assignment. Guys like John Havlicek, Walt Frazier, and Jerry West didn't scare him off. He's been nothing but an asset to our team."

What Archibald demonstrated that first year was his amazing ability to control a basketball with his dribbling. It was a part of his game that he worked on endlessly on the playgrounds of the Bronx. Archibald could dribble with either hand and was hard to defend against. If you played him to his right, he would switch hands and dribble with his left hand. Or vice versa. He never once has to look at the ball while he's dribbling. He has that much control after years of working at it.

Often he'll bait his opponent. He'll stand out there 25 to 30 feet from the basket dribbling. It looks so easy to take the ball away. Most defenders try and come away empty-handed. But that's the way Archibald has it figured. Quick as a flash, he dribbles past his man and either goes in

**Little Nate swoops in to score on an underhand lay-up.**

for a lay-up or passes off to an open teammate.

That's the secret of Archibald's game. He prefers to go one-on-one with an opponent, daring him to take the ball away from him. Archibald will jockey for position and then—swoosh—make a move for the basket. He's just too quick to keep up with. That quickness more than anything else makes up for his lack of height.

"I feel I can draw a foul almost every time," said Archibald. "You would think that the big man has an advantage, but I claim I have it because he has his arms up high and he has to come down on you. I go right for the big man and make him commit himself, then I make my move.

"On the fast breaks I like to hurry upcourt with the ball. I primarily try to draw the defense out so I can get the ball to either of the forwards, whoever is open. If they don't protect the basket, then I try to go all the way.

"That's why being able to pass properly is very important to little guys like me. It is up to us to get the ball to the open man or to start a play accurately. Passing is a skill I worked on along with my dribbling. It's that necessary if you want to become a top guard. Sometimes I pass too hard just to keep the defense from stealing the ball. But I guess sometimes when I'm going to the basket my teammates assume that I'm going all the way in and when I pass off at the last minute they aren't ready for it. That is going to happen though. It happens to me too, at times.

"But all the time I am dribbling, hoping to make things happen, I am always looking around. Seeing all over the court is very important to a guard. If he is going to be the quarterback of the offense and help to account for a basket with a pass to someone close to the basket, he has to always be alert."

Yet before the 1971-72 season, the Royals seriously considered trading Archibald to the Chicago Bulls. The Royals lacked a big center and they wanted to trade Archibald to the Bulls for center Tom Boerwinkle. The trade didn't happen and, looking back, Cousy was glad he didn't complete it. Archibald showed he was too good to lose.

When the season began, Cousy told Archibald that he wanted him to be the floor leader, which was the role Cousy played with the great Celtic teams. Archibald didn't let Cousy down. He averaged 28.2 points a game, second only to Kareem Abdul-Jabbar of the Milwaukee Bucks. Archibald became a name around the league.

By his third pro season in 1972-73, Archibald was a sensation. He made a clean sweep of almost every NBA category. He led the league in scoring with a fantastic 34-point average, which was the highest average ever achieved by a guard, surpassing Oscar Robertson's 1963-64 mark of 31 points a game. He just missed beating

Robertson's 11.5 assists-a-game record by averaging 11.4.

But the tireless Archibald was the first guard since Slater Martin in 1955-56 to lead the league in playing time with 3,681 minutes for the season. Cousy, a former guard himself, marveled at his star playmaker.

Archibald broke through with honors. He was named to the NBA All-Pro first team and was selected Player of the Year by *The Sporting News*. But the one honor that Archibald and many others felt he should have received—the NBA's Most Valuable Player—escaped him. Archibald finished third behind Abdul-Jabbar and Boston's Dave Cowens, two big centers. But Archibald didn't complain.

"I just felt good leading the league in so many categories," he remarked. "Besides, I had proven my point, that a little man can play this game and do well at it. My main concern now is helping our team win a few more games and getting into the playoffs."

During the early part of the 1973-74 campaign, Archibald suffered a severe injury. He ripped the Achilles tendon in his foot and his leg was placed in a cast for six weeks. To work his way back into shape, Archibald undertook a vigorous training program. He jogged seven miles a day and lifted weights with his leg. Later he discovered that it helped maintain his stamina. Through sheer determination, Archibald made it back, overcoming an injury that has ended the careers of other players.

Determination has always been a Tiny Archibald trademark. Early in his pro career, he had a habit of overhandling the ball, throwing it away and taking poor shots. It resulted in numerous turnovers. Archibald had to learn to slow things down. Even then, he was still faster and quicker than most of the other guards around the league. He just had to learn to pace himself more, which was no reflection on his ability. Opposing players recognized that Archibald was something special.

"I learned early that to make it in pro ball takes part skill and the other part determination. You gotta fight all the way. That's what I try to teach kids today. They need help, someone to show them the way." That's how unselfish Nate Archibald is.

The Nets' fans are delighted that Tiny is now a permanent New Yorker.

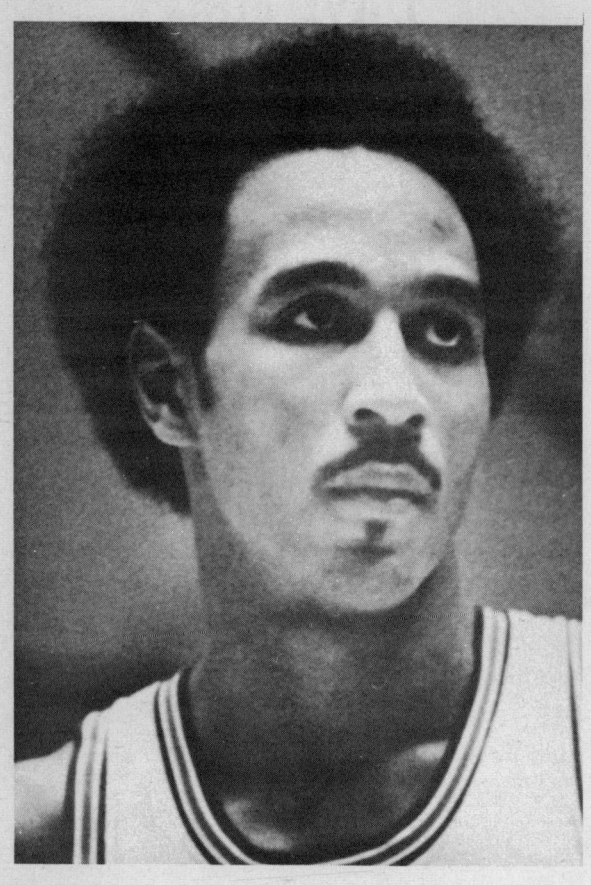

**Dave Bing: Piston play-maker and all-around performer.**

# DAVE BING
# The Come-Back Kid

It looked like any other All-Star game. Only this time there was a bit of controversy surrounding Washington's veteran guard Dave Bing prior to the 1976 contest in Philadelphia. A lot of people felt there were a great many other guards around the NBA who were better than Bing at the time.

After the first half ended, there were plenty of others who thought Bing didn't deserve a place on the team. The East was behind 50-45, and Bing hadn't scored a single point. The West stars were in control and things didn't look good for the East, not the way little Nate Archibald and big Kareem Abdul-Jabbar were playing. Archibald was controlling the ball and Jabbar was controlling the rebounds.

Before the third quarter began, East coach Tom Heinsohn came up with some new strategy. He realized that Bing's best game is to go one-on-one with his opponent, in this case Archibald. He instructed Bing to take Archibald into the pivot on offense in an effort to bottle him up and keep him from leading the fast break. Bing liked the idea.

"I have always believed in going one-on-one with my man," said Bing. "It's my type of game. I can best make things happen that way."

Not everybody can work a one-on-one situation as well as Bing. The 6-1 Bing is faster than most of the other guards and a lot quicker, too. He drives to the basket better than most others.

What makes Bing so effective in this maneuver is a combination of things. First, he is an excellent dribbler who knows how to control the ball, dribbling to his left or right and keeping the ball away from his opponent. When Bing decides to make his move toward the basket, his teammates clear the way for him by moving to the other side of the floor. It gives Bing more room to operate.

Because he is also an excellent passer, Bing is that much more effective in going one-on-one. When dribbling up the middle, Bing likes to split the defenses. Then, once past his defender, Bing will go high in the air, take the shot if it's there, or pass off to a free teammate on either side of him for an easy basket.

"It's tough going one-on-one almost every night, but I enjoy the challenge," admits Bing. "I get as much satisfaction passing off for an easy basket as I do in making one. It serves to prove that my style of play in that particular situation created a basket."

Bing is much faster than he appears. He has a long-striding drive that gets him there quicker than most. His ability to accelerate gives him an edge on any opponent who is not alert.

The cool-looking Bing is not a maniac on the court, wildly running up and down. Rather, he takes the fast break only if it's there. That's another reason why he has so much control.

"The fast break is the quickest way to the basket, but not if you have to force it," said Bing. "Forcing the ball will only result in turning it over, and that's taking two points away from you and giving the other guy a chance to make two points himself.

"That was one of the biggest adjustments I had to make when I came into the NBA, to learn to control the ball and not carelessly give it up. It's a lot different than college ball."

So Bing controlled the ball against Archibald in the All-Star game and it worked. The tactic not only slowed Archibald down, but it opened up Bing on the attack. Bing hit for 10 points in the third quarter and pushed the East to a 76-69 lead. He was the spark the East needed.

Bing broke open the close game in the fourth quarter by adding six more points before he was taken out of the game. The East won easily, 123-109, and Bing finished with 16 points and four assists. He was voted the game's most valuable player by a wide margin over Buffalo's Bob

MacAdoo, 43 to 13. Bing certainly fulfilled the faith the fans had placed in him.

"Getting the trophy was icing on the cake," said Bing. "When I arrived for the game, the Most Valuable Player award never crossed my mind. All I wanted to do was play well and be on the winning squad. In an All-Star game, nobody wants to hog the show. Winning the MVP is great because this is a game of stars and to be voted MVP makes you a star of stars. But for me, the big thing to win comes at the end of the season, the NBA championship."

That's what the Bullets had in mind when they traded for Bing. They felt he would be the missing link in winning a championship. Washington would make it to the playoffs, sometimes to the finals, but could never win it all. When they got Bing from the Pistons, it shocked Detroit fans. Bing had his greatest years in Detroit and was a big favorite there.

And yet, the Pistons never really wanted Bing when they drafted him in 1966, despite the fact that he averaged 25 points a game in his three years at Syracuse University. They desperately wanted Cazzie Russell, a star forward at the University of Michigan. However, they lost a coin toss with the New York Knickerbockers for the right to select first that year. The Knicks picked Russell and the Pistons disappointedly chose Bing.

It wasn't the first time Bing had to prove himself. He had to prove himself ever since he was a kid. He was raised in the northeast part of Washington, the ghetto, and when you're small, as Bing was, it's that much tougher. His first experience with pain was when he was five years old. He found two sticks, nailed them together, and pretended it was a horse. Happily, he rode down the street until he tripped and one of the nails plunged into his left eye. Only an operation saved his sight.

"My father was a bricklayer and his work was seasonal," said Bing. "He got laid off in the winter. My mother worked as a domestic when he didn't work. I used to go on construction jobs with my father. I saw men have their fingers chopped off by elevators. My brother saw a scaffold of men fall. A brick crashed four stories and hit my father in the head. It crushed his helmet. He had a blood clot on the brain. They thought he wouldn't pull through, but he did. I swore right then and there that I'd never live a life like that."

So Bing turned to sports as an escape. He loved sports, especially basketball. But, because he was so small, the other kids wouldn't let him play with them in the school playgrounds. It was very frustrating, so Bing turned to baseball as a release. When he went to Springarn High School, he met Dr. William Roundtree, the basketball coach. He worked with Bing, encouraged him, and was like an extra father to him. Bing gives him credit for molding him into what he became.

Still, Bing was a bit insecure about his basketball ability. He had offers from UCLA and Michigan, two strong basketball colleges. Yet when the time came, he selected Syracuse. He figured it would be a lot easier to make it big on a so-so team.

He became a star and in a most unusual way. He got married after his freshman year to his girlfriend who came up from Washington. Bing was only 19 and his wife was only 17. After a year, Bing had a baby daughter to support, and then a second daughter. He took a job as a custodian at night, scrubbing floors until 10 P.M. and studying until midnight. He also wanted to help other kids. So he found time to go into Syracuse's black neighborhood, ran clinics for the kids, and told them not to smoke or drink and above all to stay out of trouble.

In his rookie season with Detroit, Bing had a hot scoring hand with 1,601 points. He was the sixth rookie in NBA history to go over 1,600 points. Bing was easily named the league's Rookie of the Year. But it was still a year of learning for Bing. He had to learn about the physical part of defense, something he was unfamiliar with in college.

The two other Piston guards, Eddie Miles and

**Perfect timing enables Bing to swipe rebound from foe.**

Tom Van Arsdale, who were bigger and more physical than Bing, worked on him. They'd rough him up on drives and intimidate him with their hands. Then Miles would take him to the playgrounds for more work. Miles would belt him with his arm and hip when Bing tried to dribble. Then he'd trip him, hold him, and lean on him, always making him aware of the contact. But Bing learned and learned well.

In his second year, Bing led the NBA in scoring with a 27.1 average. Elgin Baylor of the Los Angeles Lakers was the only other player to score over 2,000 points. Bing dribbled around his defenders, crashed the boards, and hung high in the air driving for the basket. He was mixing it up with the big guys even though it cost him physically. In four different eye injuries, Bing wound up with a total of 32 stitches, not including five more on his nose in another injury. He also broke his left thumb for the second time, but kept right on playing as if nothing happened.

But his biggest scare occurred just before the 1971 season. He was scratched in the eye by Happy Hairston and rushed to the hospital where an operation was ordered for a detached retina. Following the operation, he lay in darkness for days, wondering if he would ever see again.

"That was the scariest time of my life," he recalls. "Three days after the operation they took off the patches. It really was a tremendous feeling when I knew I would be able to see again.

"Yet I honestly didn't know if I could play basketball again. I didn't know if I could see out of the corner of my eye, let alone see in front of me to shoot and pass. The doctors were skeptical about my playing basketball. They were afraid it might happen again and warned me that I might lose my sight in that eye altogether.

"But it was my fifth year of pro ball and I didn't want to quit while I was approaching the top of my game. I loved the game too much to quit then. It was my whole life. It was a risk, but so far it's turned out okay."

Bing spent three more years in Detroit, helping the club to its best record ever in 1973-74. Then after a dissension-riddled 1974-75 season, Detroit traded Bing to Washington for Kevin Porter. The Pistons also gave up their number-one draft choice to get the flashy Porter. The Piston fans still didn't like it.

"It was a change for me to go to another organization," revealed Bing. "The only thing I could add to the Bullets was a championship, since they'd already gone to the finals. Sure, I felt the pressure at the beginning."

It took time for Bing to make the adjustment. But midway during the season, he finally felt comfortable.

"When he came to this team he tried to be Kevin Porter," observed Bullet star Elvin Hayes. "He didn't have to be Kevin. He's a great player and an All-Star. All he had to be was Dave Bing."

No one could have put it better.

# JO JO WHITE
# The Take-Charge Guy

The fifth game of the 1975-76 National Basketball Association championship finals will never be forgotten by Boston's Jo Jo White, let alone countless more who watched the game on television. In excitement alone, the game had no equal.

The home team Celtics and the Phoenix Suns, who were in the championships for the first time, were involved in the most dramatic game in playoff history. It was a key game, too. Boston and Phoenix had split the first four games, each winning two, in the best-of-seven series to determine the NBA championship. Whoever would win the pivotal fifth game would have a 3-2 advantage. More important, the winners would walk away with a big psychological edge, knowing they would have to win only one more game to become champions. Jo Jo White, the solid, 6-3 veteran guard of the Celtics, realized it more than anyone else.

"I thought a long time about what had happened after we lost the second game to Phoenix,"

Jo Jo White: one of NBA's deadliest clutch shooters.

said White. "I realized it was going to take even more effort than we originally thought, but if we could win, it would mean even more."

White was the deciding factor in the crucial fifth game, one which was tied at 95-95 in regulation play. With four seconds left in the first overtime, White stole the ball from Ricky Sobers to preserve the 101-101 tie.

In the second overtime, White scored seven of Boston's 11 points. His biggest came with one second left when he sank a pressure foul shot that gave the Celtics a 112-110 lead. It was a big point, because Gar Heard made a miraculous jumper that tied the score at 112-112 as the buzzer sounded.

Both teams were tired when the third overtime period began. Twice White brought the Celtics from behind with key baskets that tied the score at 116-116 and 118-118. Then he fed McDonald with a quick pass underneath which resulted in a basket that put Boston on top, 120-118. A short time later he hit on a one-hander that gave the Celtics a 124-120 edge with only 55 seconds remaining. And finally, to top off his efforts, White dribbled out the clock to preserve the Celtics' 128-126 triumph.

White had scored 15 of his team's 33 points in the overtime. In his long night's work, he made 15 of 29 field-goal attempts, had nine assists, and finished with 33 points.

The victory was like a vitamin pill. It gave the Celtics a 3-2 lead in games. And just two days later in Phoenix, the Celtics won the championship quite easily.

At the conclusion of the game, White was named the Most Valuable Player of the playoffs. And it wasn't because he was the Celtics' leading scorer with 130 points. He was a major contributor on defense, so much so that his play enabled the Celtics to win the opening game of the series, 98-87.

Boston coach Tom Heinsohn made an important decision that clearly affected the game. Instead of letting Charlie Scott guard Paul Westphal, the Suns' leading scorer, he decided that White should watch him. It was a very big move. Scott had guarded Westphal every time the two clubs met during the regular season. Switching at this point put a lot of pressure on White. However, it didn't upset him one bit. White did a remarkable job on defense. Westphal could only hit on four of 17 field-goal attempts as he finished with only eight points.

Yet it took the dramatic fifth game to earn White the recognition he deserved. In fact, it proved what Heinsohn felt about White's ability all along.

"I knew from the first time I saw him that Jo Jo White would be a great, great basketball player," said Heinsohn. "He's finally getting the recognition he deserves. He's done everything I've ever asked him to do and if I told him to go out and run through a wall for us to win, you can be sure he'd give it three good cracks. He's been our foundation and he's grown every year as a player. He's been a starter for us every year. He may become our all-time leading scorer. His ability to do all the things asked of him has been the basis of our success. He's a true Celtic and his day has come. No one's played more consistently or reliably, and he runs the break better than almost anybody. Need I continue?"

Being named the Most Valuable Player in the championship series brought a great amount of satisfaction to White. A quiet person, White doesn't make his feelings known very often. He just quietly does what's expected of him. Maybe that's why he hasn't drawn much attention to his contributions on the court.

"I never thought that in my career I'd see the day when I'd be an MVP," remarked White. "I saw myself as the ghetto kid from St. Louis trying to improve myself as best I could. But I saw the MVP awards going to the big men and the great ones in the league. Finally, however, they've recognized the smaller man."

There is no finer all-around guard in the NBA today than White. He is solid, not flashy, in all aspects of the game—passing, dribbling, shooting, setting up plays, defense, and awareness of what is taking place on both ends of the court.

He is a tireless worker who shows no emotion during a game. Rather, he coolly produces in his role as the quarterback of Boston's high-powered offense that often begins when White takes an outlet pass and starts the famed Celtic fast break in motion.

To do this, White must have complete control. That requires total vision of the action not only in front of him but all around him. He has to know exactly how deep he can take his dribble, when to pass off to either one of his teammates running alongside, or to shoot the ball himself. And he has to make his decision in a split second. His wide-angle vision (called peripheral vision) is legendary in the NBA. "He's like a fly," says one coach. "His eyes can catch movement on all sides."

White demonstrated in the playoffs just how important condition is to a little man. Because he is constantly on the move, a guard must be in better shape than anyone else. Otherwise, White wouldn't have lasted three overtimes and still become the deciding factor in Boston's victory.

Nobody realizes it more than White. He doesn't wait for training camp to start getting into shape. About a month after the season ends, White begins to jog every day to build up his wind and stamina. After the jogging, he runs a couple of miles every day at a brisk pace.

Even as a kid growing up in St. Louis White felt

the need to produce. He was the seventh, and last, child of Rev. George and Mrs. Elizabeth White, and Jo Jo kiddingly remarks that he grew up on the "front part of the south side ghetto."

Still, he remembers the neighborhood as "fun" to grow up in, even though he experienced some tough times with other kids. But nothing ever serious. He got involved with sports, mainly through an older brother and a cousin. But White didn't play basketball. Instead, he took up football. He was deeply involved with football until a hand injury scared his mother. She quickly warned him to give it up.

It wasn't until he was 11 years old that he got interested in basketball at a recreation center. He found the game natural to him. And he loved it. So much so, that his father was openly skeptical that Jo Jo was shooting baskets until 11 and 12 midnight. White admits he never could convince his father that he was at the rec-center all that time.

But it all paid off. His father was finally convinced when he saw White play in his first high school freshman game. He realized then that Jo Jo did indeed put in a lot of time at the rec-center all those nights. Three years later he was All-City and was offered an athletic scholarship to Kansas University.

Some of his friends tried to convince him that Kansas wasn't the best place for him. They pointed out that Kansas played a type of game built around the forwards and center. But White handled it, earned All-America honors, and played in the 1968 Pan American and Olympic Games.

The Celtics, who picked ninth on the first round of the 1969 college draft, were happy to get him. The only reason he was so low in the draft was because most of the other teams thought that White would have to spend two years in military service. However, White spent six months with the Marines and joined the Celtics in November. It was Heinsohn's first year as coach and the club was struggling when White reported.

The first thing Heinsohn told White to do was shoot. This was something new to White. At Kansas, he played control ball, setting up the forwards and center. And that's what White concentrated on doing in the 60 pro games he played his rookie season. He averaged 12.2 points and there was plenty of room for improvement.

In 1970-71, White averaged 21.3 points a game; in 1971-72, 23.1 points a game; in 1972-73, 19.7 points a game, and in 1973-74, 18.1 points a game. But still, the Celtics weren't getting the most out of White's all-around abilities. He was more than just a shooter.

The turning point in White's development as a complete player came early in the 1974-75 season. The Celtics were experiencing trouble winning. They had lost five of their last eight games and

**White sees an opening and starts a drive toward net.**

were 11-10 on the season, which is far from championship ball. Heinsohn called a closed-door meeting which lasted two hours as the players got a lot off their chests. No one benefited more from that meeting than White.

"In the meeting we decided that I would run the offense and call the plays," White disclosed. "I have to think about doing it every game. I can't have a lapse. It's like a quarterback in football. Everybody's counting on him to be there. My job has changed so much with this club. First they wanted me to score and then it was something else.

"If I have the ability to do more than one thing, I should be able to do it. That's why we decided I'd run the offense. I feel I'm a better player when I have a definite job. I carry it out better and it makes it a lot easier because I've always been a quarterback out there. If I'm hot, then I'll call my plays and take my shots. But I usually call plays for everyone. It makes our offense better. It's the team way and I've always played like that."

White performs without a problem in his new role. He glides up the court with deceiving speed. His play selection is excellent because of his awareness of what is taking place. He does it all. He makes the fast break go. If he doesn't pass off on a set play, he will stop and pop his jump shot with amazing accuracy. He is the playmaker and the scorer. He has to call the necessary plays and still be ready to drive for the basket if needed. And all the time, he is also asked to play defense, going 40 minutes a game. Which he does. In four seasons, from 1972 through 1976, White has never missed a game.

"Jo Jo was never super flashy," pointed out Heinsohn, "and I think that's something the press has always wanted him to be, which, of course, is unfair."

It's a good thing, too. If White was super flashy, he'd probably turn out to be Superman!

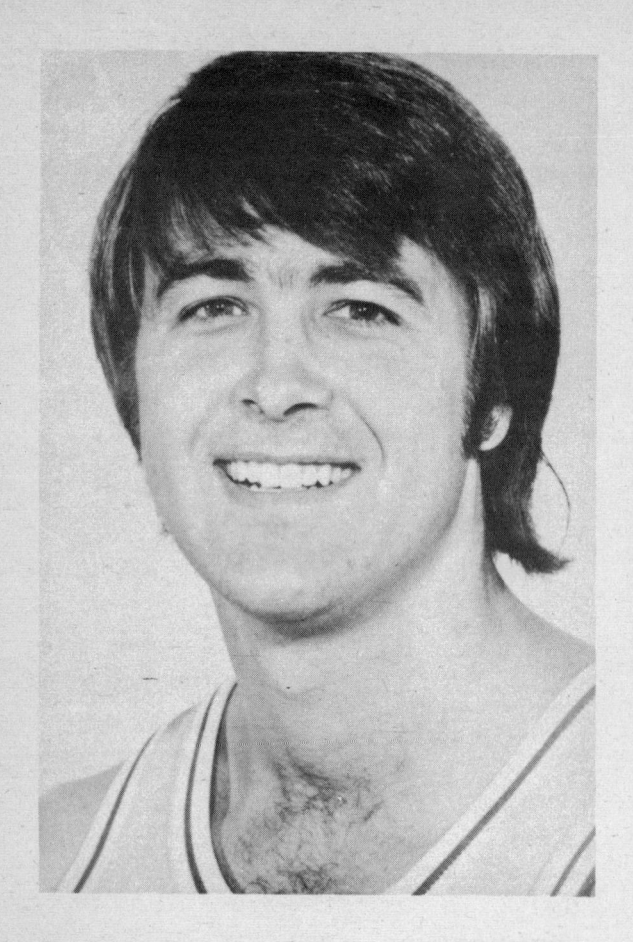

**Gail Goodrich: now pairs up with Jazz's Pete Maravich.**

# GAIL GOODRICH
## He Does It All

Gail Goodrich could feel the pressure night after night. During the 1975-76 season, the veteran 6-1 guard of the Los Angeles Lakers played without a contract. To many people, it didn't appear a serious situation. After all, Goodrich had been a Laker for nine of his 11 seasons in the NBA. Most everyone felt that Goodrich would have another good year and sign another contract with the Lakers... only this time for a lot more money.

Goodrich did have another fine season. He averaged 19.5 points a game, second best on the team and 19th among the league's scorers, and he topped the Lakers in assists with an average of 5.6 a game, which was eighth best in the NBA. Goodrich had shown that at the age of 32 he had not slowed down.

He also showed he was as quick off the court as he is on it. Instead of signing with the Lakers as most people had expected, Goodrich signed with the New Orleans Jazz as a free agent.

The move shocked Lakers fans, since Goodrich was one of the most popular players on the squad. At the same time, Goodrich's move brought a great amount of joy to followers of the Jazz. In signing with New Orleans, Goodrich joins another star at guard, "Pistol" Pete Maravich. Together, they represent the biggest backcourt scoring punch in the NBA.

In the 1975-76 season, Maravich averaged 25.9 points a game, third best in the NBA. Together with Goodrich, the Jazz can expect an average of 45 points a game from these two players alone. In fact, the presence of Goodrich might realize even more point production. Opposing teams can't concentrate on stopping Maravich, like they did in the past, with Goodrich around.

"Gail is a shooter, but he prefers to play without the ball," pointed out Jazz general manager Barry Mendelson. "He is perhaps the best guard in the league in moving without the ball. He's always moving. He shoots better when he comes off the ball and sets a screen for a teammate. Gail has an accurate jump shot from outside. We're happy we got him."

And Goodrich was happy to sign with the Jazz. It provided him with peace of mind and relieved a lot of pressure inside of him.

"I didn't want to go through another season like

I experienced in 1975-76," said Goodrich. "Mentally, it was very tough. The Lakers were going through a big change. The players were constantly changing. It created a great deal of confusion. It makes it tough to adjust.

"I signed with the Jazz with the intention of making the playoffs. In their second year during the 1975-76 season, they won 38 games, only two less than the Lakers. I figure I can add that much more and make the playoffs. It's a great challenge and I certainly hope I can help make the team a winner."

Goodrich is used to a challenge. Born in Los Angeles, Goodrich was only 5-11 when he played at Poly High School. In his senior year, he led Poly to the city title and was named player of the year. Despite his size, Goodrich was sought by many California colleges. His father had been a basketball star at the University of Southern California, UCLA's chief rival. Naturally, USC felt that Goodrich would follow his father's footsteps. However, Goodrich decided to play for perhaps college basketball's greatest coach, John Wooden of UCLA.

Goodrich led UCLA's freshmen team to a perfect 20-0 season in 1961. When he reported to the varsity, Goodrich was almost 6-1 and his teammates had named him "The Twig" and "Mr. Quick." And with good reason. Goodrich had fast hands and quick reflexes. In a split second he could steal the ball out of his opponent's hands.

But he also had another knack. Wooden observed that Goodrich had an uncanny sense of timing when it came to getting rebounds. Although he couldn't jump with the bigger forwards underneath the basket, Goodrich would often come away with the ball. He had a sixth sense in pulling off a rebound. What he did was correctly anticipate where the ball would bounce off the rim, quickly slip past his opponent and end up with the ball.

For this ability alone, Wooden regularly used Goodrich as a forward. He would draw cheers from the crowd when he would grab a rebound and in a split second quickly throw it up for a basket.

But it was in the backcourt that Goodrich truly excelled. Because of his quickness, he led the Bruins' nifty fast break. He would take a pass and quickly lead the Bruins' attack, either shooting himself with a rapid one-hand jump shot or passing off.

He was also valuable on defense. With his quick hands, Goodrich was a key factor in UCLA's famous trap press. Goodrich would crowd his opponent and either force him into a turnover or leave him completely frustrated by knocking the ball out of his hands.

The Lakers had watched and waited for Goodrich for three years until they made him their

**Famed for off-balance acrobatics, Goodrich pumps it up.**

number-one draft pick in 1965. However, they traded him to Phoenix in 1968, but realized their mistake and got him back in 1970.

Goodrich enjoyed six good years with the Lakers. He played with Jerry West, Elgin Baylor, Wilt Chamberlain, and Kareem Abdul-Jabbar and won a championship in 1972.

During the 1973-74 season, Goodrich had his greatest year as a pro. He led the Lakers in scoring with a 25.3 average and in assists with 5.2. The season was personally gratifying to Goodrich, because for years all he heard was that he was a much better player when teaming with Jerry West in the backcourt. Together, they were an excellent combination. It's no wonder that opposing teams will now shudder at the thought of Goodrich and Maravich playing together.

Being only 6-1, Goodrich works hard for his points. Extremely quick for his size, he has the ability to get open. He employs this tactic when he doesn't have the ball. What he does is take his opponent away from the action and then quickly make a move toward the ball or the basket. Playing alongside Maravich, Goodrich has more opportunity to make use of this part of his game. Besides being an excellent shooter, Maravich is a fancy passer, which allows him to play give-and-go with Goodrich.

When he has the ball, Goodrich is a strong dribbler. His quickness enables him to drive around his opponent, especially when he is guarded too closely. He doesn't hesitate to shoot his accurate left-hand jump shot from practically any spot on the court. That's what keeps his opponents off balance. If they slack off to guard against his drive, then Goodrich will pop to make them play him tighter. Then when they crowd him, he doesn't hesitate to make his quick move toward the basket.

Goodrich does this well. Although he is short, he has long arms (a 37-inch shirtsleeve). He uses this advantage inside to slip around or shoot over whoever is guarding him. Goodrich also has the knack to hang in mid-air, pumping the ball once or twice before shooting, making him tough to defend. It's one reason why Goodrich draws so many fouls.

The only rap hanging over his head is the fact that some consider Goodrich a bit weak on defense. He's had to live with the accusation since his first year in the league in 1965. The statement is not exactly fair, because Goodrich's offensive skills have overshadowed his defensive play. It doesn't bother Goodrich.

"If you compare my defense to my offense, it's obviously not as good," he points out. "But I think my defense is better than people give me credit for. Sure, people say that I don't play defense. But I don't see a lot of guys scoring 30 points on me. And the ones who do are scoring on everyone else, too. Of course, I'm not taking on the real tough big guard 6-4 or more. I think I got this bad-defense label when I came into the league way back, and it's been difficult to shake."

When he was with the Lakers, Goodrich always displayed consistency. In 1974-75, he led the Lakers in points scored and shooting average for the fourth straight time, despite missing 10 games with injuries. He scored 1,630 points for an average of 22.6 and topped the club in assists for the second straight year with an average of 5.8. It was no fault of Goodrich's that the Lakers missed getting into the playoffs for the first time in five years.

The same season, Goodrich enjoyed his biggest night as a pro by scoring 53 points against the Kansas City-Omaha Kings. Even Goodrich himself had no idea he would finish the game with so many points. He scored only 17 points the first half but really got hot and exploded with 36 points in the final half. He finished the game with 21 of 38 field goal attempts and 11 of 12 from the foul line. During the game, he also went over the 15,000 career-points mark. Only four Lakers before him had scored 50 points in a single game: Wilt Chamberlain, Elgin Baylor, Rudy LaRusso, and Jerry West.

"I like to believe I'm a better shooter now than earlier in my career even though my percentage may not be as high," Gail says. "This is because my shot-selection isn't as good when the team is looking for me to score more.

"There is something else. I'm getting better at getting my shots. There's a difference between a pure shooter and a scorer. For example, I don't consider John Havlicek a pure shooter, but he gets open to score. I would like to believe I'm a shooter and scorer.

"I get down on myself when I have bad games. I don't accept bad games. I think I should play at a top level every night and, when I don't, I get very upset. I know I'm going to have off nights, but I just don't accept them. If you look at my history, I've been a player who is as active without the ball as with it. One season, I was fourth in the league in assists, which is difficult for some people to believe."

One thing that Jazz fans believe now is that in Goodrich and Maravich, they have the strongest backcourt scoring punch in the NBA. Nobody can argue with them, either.

# CALVIN MURPHY
# Mighty Mite With Clout

The challenge was there right from the beginning. Calvin Murphy knew it. He had to prove that he belonged. He had to show everyone that he wasn't too small to play professional basketball. But the challenge wasn't easy. Not when you're only 5-9 and you are going against Wilt Chamberlain, who is an awesome 7-1. That's what Murphy was up against. But he wasn't about to back down. Too much was at stake, possibly his entire career. He had to meet the challenge and overcome it. Only Murphy knew at the time how important the moment was.

Just before the 1970-71 season, the then San Diego Rockets faced the Los Angeles Lakers in an exhibition game. Although he had looked good in training camp, Murphy still hadn't fully convinced many people that he wasn't too small to play in the NBA. Chamberlain wasn't about to offer him any encouragement. Instead, he gave Murphy a warning.

**Calvin Murphy: Rocket ace may own fastest hands of all.**

"If you want to stay on the court, rookie, then stay out of the middle," growled Chamberlain.

The message was clear. If Murphy tried to operate in the middle, then Chamberlain would stuff the ball down his throat. Wilt frequently did such things to players much taller than Murphy. For a moment, Murphy thought about Chamberlain's warning. Should he stay away from Chamberlain's area or should he play his normal game—driving down the middle for a jump shot or a lay-up? Against someone five or six inches taller, Murphy wouldn't have too much trouble. But against Chamberlain, who was more than a foot bigger, and known for his defense, the task would be extremely difficult. In fact, it was an over-match.

Murphy decided to challenge Wilt. He felt he had to prove to his teammates and coach Alex Hannum that he could play pro ball. The odds were against Murphy, but he was willing to take them to prove his point. A few minutes later, the challenge presented itself. Murphy dribbled around his man and headed down the middle. Chamberlain came out to meet him. Murphy faked one way; Wilt, fooled, went the other way. As the crowd cheered, Murphy followed his fake to go in for an easy lay-up as Chamberlain could only turn and look as the ball went through the basket.

The play showed one important thing. Despite

his size, Murphy would not be intimidated, not by Chamberlain or anybody else for that matter. About a week later, Mel Counts, the seven-foot center of the Phoenix Suns, found out that Murphy wouldn't back away from a challenge. In the opening game of the season, Murphy drove toward the basket and went up against the big man. Again the crowd roared as Murphy soared high in the air and scored a basket by shooting over the taller Counts. Murphy showed that he belonged.

"Calvin has a bit of a handicap in his jumping," smiled Hannum afterwards. "It takes him so long to come down."

Yet, there was a time when the pro scouts weren't so convinced about Murphy's ability. At Niagara University, Murphy was a bona fide All-American. He finished with a 33.1 career average, fourth highest on the NCAA record books. Only Pete Maravich, Oscar Robertson, and Austin Carr managed to average higher than Murphy. However, in the 1970 college draft, Murphy was the only All-American who wasn't drafted on the first round. Murphy was stunned by the snub. So much so that he seriously considered signing a big contract with the Harlem Magicians.

"They said I was too small to play in high school," exclaimed Murphy, "and I made All-America three straight years. Now they say I can't play in the pros. Well, I know I can."

Two things influenced Murphy to sign with the Rockets and reject the Magicians' contract even though it offered more money. The first was Willis Reed, the former New York Knickerbocker star who was a friend of Murphy's. The other went way back to his childhood when Murphy, growing up and playing in Norwalk, Conn., dreamed about playing in the NBA.

"I played a lot of ball with the pros at summer camps and clinics," recalled Murphy. "I handled myself pretty well, too. I was confident I could play NBA ball. In fact, I wanted to be a superstar. I felt I had the things needed to achieve that status."

Murphy earned this sort of confidence by himself. He had to battle his lack of height as well as poverty. It took a lot of hard work but Murphy was willing to make the sacrifice. Although he did have a great amount of natural ability, Murphy was clumsy as a youngster. But he overcame his clumsiness by playing ball practically all day every day for years.

It is his unique jumping ability that makes Murphy actually taller than he is. Realizing that he wouldn't ever be tall, Murphy worked extra hard as a youngster to develop his jumping ability. To increase his strength, he wore heavy work boots in his jumping work-outs. There were many days when he shoveled the snow off the playground courts just to practice by himself. His determination paid off, too. Now, he can actually jump against a player several inches taller.

Along with his knack to spring off the floor, Murphy also developed an excellent jump shot. He realized that most of his points would have to come away from the basket. So, with his heavy work boots on, Murphy would jump high and pop one-handers until he was all tired out.

Murphy has great ball control. Because of his ability to leap high, he must hold on to the ball longer than most guards. His strong wrists enable him to either fire a pass in mid-air or shoot a jump shot, seemingly without effort. As a youngster he developed strong wrists by twirling a baton. He was so good at it that he was national baton twirling champion his freshman year at Niagara University.

Because of his leaping ability, Murphy isn't afraid to drive to the basket despite his size. He makes it work to his advantage. He'll either try to drive around his opponent or stop quickly, go up high, and get off a jump shot.

"I know what I'm going to do because I'm in control," said Murphy. "It's up to my opponent to try and guess what I'm going to do—whether I'll drive all the way or stop and pop a jumper.

"I thought I would grow to be a lot bigger when I was a kid. My whole family was big, one brother was 6-3 and the other was 6-4. But by the time I reached the ninth grade, I knew I wasn't going to grow. So, I stopped worrying. I just tried to do the best I could with what I had.

"My friends, of all people, used to discourage me. Like when I went to high school, they said I was too small to make the basketball team. I tried out anyway. I made All-State my sophomore year."

In his rookie pro year, Hannum brought Murphy along slowly. He averaged 24 minutes of playing time a game, which was exactly half a game. It was a strange role for Murphy because he had always played a full game and was counted on to supply the points. Now he had to learn it all, playing good defense and hitting the open man with a pass on offense. Nevertheless, he managed to average 15.8 points a game while playing only half the time. Murphy proved that he belonged in pro ball.

Despite his size, Murphy is strong physically, which compensates for his shortness. His well-defined muscles alone give him an appearance of power. His wrists and shoulders are especially strong and he has great spring in his legs. These assets provide Murphy with one of the best jump shots in pro basketball. When Murphy goes up for a jumper, he hangs in space for what seems an eternity. It enables him to get his jump shot off without it being blocked by taller opponents.

In traffic, Murphy moves with darting speed. He has excellent body control to go along with his

**Murphy protects ball with quick shift to lefty dribble.**

quickness. It enables him to move through openings that bigger players could not maneuver. Certainly there isn't anybody in the league who can move toward the basket faster than Murphy. Offensively, Murphy's skills were evident.

Defensively, Murphy had to make much more of an adjustment. He couldn't allow the taller guards, when they were on offense, to take him underneath the basket. To discourage this, Murphy likes to pick up his opponent at mid-court and stay close to him. He harrasses him all the way downcourt, seeking to keep his opponent out of shooting range. He thinks nothing of scrambling, crowding, grabbing, or pushing, and therefore at times gets into foul trouble. But at the same time, his aggressiveness enables him to hold his own on defense against the bigger guards.

"People make a lot out of how I do against the big guards," said Murphy. "I think I have one big advantage over them. They have to dribble higher and this gives me a chance to move in and steal the ball. I'm close to the ground and with my speed it's an advantage.

"All my life I've heard about the disadvantages of being small. But there are just as many advantages, too. I can squeeze through the mouse holes. If I started shying away, I'd be destroying my whole game and would have to stop and rebuild it. That's not my way. I've got to get up and get over my man.

"I'm always being knocked down. But I just pick myself up and keep going. You get used to it. If you keep asking yourself 'Why?' you might begin worrying about it. You can't be afraid."

John Brown, the 6-8 forward of the Atlanta Hawks knew what Murphy meant during the 1975-76 season. There was a brief scuffle and then Brown's big body suddenly hit the floor. Few people had seen what happened. Calvin Murphy had decked him with his fist. Nobody saw the punch, including Brown. Murphy stood over him, his fists clenched, waiting to throw more punches. But Brown didn't want any part of Murphy. Calvin's teammates restrained Murphy from doing any more battle.

"He tried to sneak-punch me as we were moving upcourt," explained Murphy after he was ejected from the game along with Brown. "But I ducked his swing, started weaving, bobbing, and swinging. And it was over so quick I didn't even know what happened."

Brown was the obvious loser. He had a black eye which was cut above the eyebrow, a bloody nose, and a cut lip. The eye needed six stitches to close.

"I've never faced anything like that whirlwind," admitted Brown. "He's so quick. He got in five or six punches before I could hit him. I want to issue a warning to other NBA forwards and centers—stay away from Murphy."

Which is all right with Murphy. However, he tried to play the fight down.

"It took that fight with Brown to make people pay attention to me again," claimed Murphy. "That's terrible. I've been in this league six years now, playing good ball, and the press hardly pays me any mind until I do something bad like getting into a fight. Hey, I'm a jump shooter, not a boxer!"

Murphy is right. He led the Rockets in scoring with a 21.0 average in 1975-76, 10th best in the NBA. He was second in free throws with a .907 percentage and third in assists with a 7.3 average. Those are All-Star credentials indeed.

"Murphy is a remarkable athlete," added Brown. "He has to be, for a guy his size to do what he does. He's proven that he belongs here."

Brown was talking about Murphy's basketball skills, not his boxing ability. Murphy doesn't have to prove anything anymore.

# NORM VAN LIER
## Thinking Big

He's not afraid of the contact. In fact, that's his style. He'll push and shove with anybody. Norm Van Lier of the Chicago Bulls has probably been on the floor more than any player in the National Basketball Association. But he's tough. Van Lier is only 6-1, but ask any big center in the NBA about Van Lier and they'll acknowledge just how tough he is. Fact is, Van Lier doesn't back down to anybody no matter how big he is. Even if they are as much as a foot taller.

One night during the 1975 season, the Bulls were playing the Detroit Pistons in a crucial game. Chicago was leading the Midwest Division race by only a single game over Detroit. A crowd of 18,836 fans turned out for the important battle, which is all the Chicago Stadium could hold. The Bulls were on a four-game winning streak and if the Pistons could beat them, the two rivals would end up tied for first place when the night was over.

**Norm Van Lier: fierce competitor won't be pushed around.**

As was expected, the game was close and tense. Early in the second quarter, Bob Lanier, the Pistons' powerful 6-11 center, began a drive to the basket. He appeared to be on his way for an easy field goal. The only person who could stop him was the much shorter Van Lier, and certainly he couldn't jump with Lanier. But what Van Lier did was gain position on Lanier and brace himself for the expected contact. Lanier barrelled into Van Lier and the little guard went sprawling on the floor. The noisy crowd moaned at the force of the impact, expecting Van Lier to be hurt. However, Van Lier got up off the floor, shook off the affects of the blow, and smiled.

Later in the game, he again challenged Lanier. Only this time Van Lier was on offense. He was on a drive under the basket and Lanier left his man in an attempt to stop Van Lier. Seeing him, Van Lier drove right to left underneath. Lanier set himself to slap away Van Lier's pass. Van Lier gave Lanier a fake and the big center jumped to block an expected pass. Instead, Van Lier took a short lefthanded shot for a basket that put the game out of reach as the Bulls went on to win, 95-83.

When the game was over, Van Lier had scored 19 points, had 11 assists, and had directed the Bulls' offense. Most of his points came at critical times. He scored four straight points at the end of the first period that cut Detroit's edge to 22-18.

He hit on a jump shot that put the Bulls ahead to stay, 49-47, and he gave his team a big edge when he scored against Lanier to make the score 63-53.

Still, the one play that ignited the Bulls, who were struggling at the time, was when Lanier charged into Van Lier knocking him on the ground. The big crowd cheered the Bulls after that.

"You can't think about taking charge," explained Van Lier after the game. "It can't be taught. It's got to be in you. I learned from football, though, that you can't think of being hurt. And you've got to make the first contact, no matter how big they are. You've got to forget how small you are and think big."

Actually, the Bulls didn't think much of Van Lier's chances to play pro ball, despite the fact that they had made him a third-round draft pick in 1969. Before the season began, the Bulls traded Van Lier to the Cincinnati Royals because he had failed to impress them during the exhibition season. They decided that he couldn't shoot, and was too small and too frail at 175 pounds. They also couldn't understand why he stood in the way and constantly got knocked down by hard-charging bigger players. That, they felt, would end his career quicker than anything else.

However, Van Lier demonstrated that he wasn't afraid to get bowled over. That he could mix and take the blows. That he was tough and aggressive. That he wasn't afraid to fight, for that matter. He proved it to the Bulls during an exhibition game the following year when Cincinnati met Chicago in a high school gym.

Van Lier and Jerry Sloan, who is a rugged 6-6 aggressive guard, began fighting underneath the basket. They went at it pretty good. They kept swinging at each other right through a set of doors that led to a hallway. They still went at it after the doors closed behind them. Although no one could see, everybody close by could hear Sloan and Van Lier pounding away at each other before the fight was finally broken up.

"We respect each other," says Van Lier. "He gives you a super effort every time he goes out. If you're on the other team, Jerry makes you want to fight him. I'll scrap for all the loose balls. Every one of them. I feel I should get them all."

No NBA backcourt man takes such physical chances as Van Lier. And it's his quickness and fast hands that add another dimension to his value. Not only will he drive recklessly for a loose ball, but he's always thinking what he can do with it when he gets it.

"Most little guys are content to just gain possession," one veteran NBA official says admiringly, "but not Van Lier. He'll dive for a ball, grab it, take a quick look and, with a lightning flick of his wrist, he'll snap it away to a teammate."

And then there are Norm's sneaky passes—

another common trick among the small, tricky guards. He'll come dribbling down furiously and suddenly spot a man he's going to pass to. His eyes and head indicate he'll be flashing the ball in that direction. But just as the man guarding him moves to cut off the pass, Van Lier's hands change the whole scene. Out of the corner of his eye he has caught another teammate cutting for the basket. Zip! The pass goes to the second man. Two points. Give the fast hands an assist.

A master dribbler, Van Lier can dribble with either hand and can change hands as he changes direction, cutting so swiftly he often catches his opponent off balance. Like many pro guards, he practiced dribbling as a small boy, with his eyes closed, learning to control the ball without looking at it as he dribbled. That's the touch that only a great ball-handler has. It's something the big men can rarely do effectively. Next time you see a game coming down to its final seconds, with a team leading by one or two points, notice who kills the clock with his dribbling; it's always the little guy with the great dribbling moves.

Van Lier brought his style of aggressiveness from Cincinnati to Chicago in 1971. The Bulls needed a floor leader and Van Lier had showed that he was certainly that. And he was perfect for the Bulls, because under coach Dick Motta Chicago had developed into the most aggressive team in the NBA. Van Lier was the spark they needed to control the offense.

The fiery Van Lier fit into Chicago's style of play with ease. He led the league in assists in 1971 and helped make the Bulls championship contenders. He also led the Bulls in technical fouls simply because his aggressive style of play led him into many heated situations, some with players and others with referees.

Back in 1972, Van Lier had a feud going with Walt Bellamy, the 6-11 center of the Atlanta Hawks. In one game, Bellamy was driving toward the basket and Van Lier cleverly got into his way. He assumed a defensive position and Bellamy was charged with an offensive foul. It annoyed Bellamy that he was intimidated by a little guy.

The next time they played against each other, it developed into a real knockdown affair. Three times Bellamy ran into Van Lier and knocked him down. Each time Bellamy grew madder. The fourth time, Bellamy crashed into Van Lier with full force. This time Van Lier didn't get up. He had to be helped to the bench somewhat dazed with a gash across his forehead. After resting a few minutes, Van Lier went back into the game as the blood trickled down the side of his head.

"You've got to make a stand," said Van Lier afterward. "If you're small, they'll take it out on you all the time. I'm not going to take that. I'll get back someway, if I have to swing with a folding chair."

In 1973, Van Lier took a stand against another big man, 6-10 John Block. Van Lier was taking the ball out of bounds when Block elbowed him. It immediately angered Van Lier. He dropped the ball and went after Block with his fists. Referee Jake O'Donnell tried to intervene and Van Lier swung at him, too. O'Donnell felt that Van Lier tried to hit him, and he did, too.

"I don't mind getting hit because the way I play I know I'm going to get that," Van Lier says. "But I'm not going to stand there and take a dirty shot from a person, because I'm not a dirty ballplayer."

But it's his defense that upsets opposing players and leads to so many scraps. Instead of allowing his opponent to gain his position, Van Lier forces him to move somewhere else. That's how Van Lier draws most of the fouls. Out of frustration, his opponent will make a reckless move to get away from Van Lier. Instead, he is called for a charging foul.

It hasn't been easy for Van Lier. His style of play has often caused problems for referees. They don't always see Van Lier's side of things and quite often the calls they make go against him. Which naturally causes Van Lier some frustra-

**Van Lier never hesitates, drives through heavy traffic.**

tion. He frequently argues with referees and hardly ever wins.

"He thinks he's being cheated on the floor or something," says O'Donnell. "He thinks because of his size he's being picked on."

But, Van Lier has a different view, one that some others agree with. Especially his fans.

"I don't get a fair shake out there," claims Van Lier. "The referees protect the superstars. I have to handle every superstar that comes into a game. They go to the foul line all the time and I'm leading the league in drawing fouls and getting thrown out of games.

"I'm handling the ball 90 percent of the time for my team and I can't get to shoot from the foul line. They protect some people. It depends on what team you're on. I play as hard as any superstar in this league. I have to. I think the superstars should worry about me instead of me worrying about them. I want them to prove to me that they are better."

Certainly no one plays the game with more intensity than Van Lier. And he has the bruised knees and elbows to prove it. Sometimes during the course of a season they balloon up and are filled with water. In later years they will probably form calcium deposits, but it doesn't worry Van Lier.

"You really get used to playing with pain," remarks Van Lier. "It doesn't hurt after awhile, although the doctors say it will some day. It's not that bad.

"But I don't think about it. If you stop to think about diving after a loose ball you wouldn't do it and you'd probably get hurt. How many times have you seen a guy make a mistake and then foul you on the next play? That's because he's thinking rather than reacting."

In 1975-76, Van Lier vowed to himself to watch his conduct and his battling the officials in order to cut down on his technical fouls. The only thing that concerned him was that in doing so, it would make him play with less intensity.

"My gripe was that I was getting beat up physically and wasn't getting any breaks," he moaned. "But it got so I was thinking more about the technicals than I was about the game. So it came to the point where I had to stop what I was doing or give up the game. I didn't want to give it up.

"So I adjusted, even out on the court. The other teams have taken the middle away from me and forced me to the outside. I hardly get a lay-up anymore. But this opens up other things. I'm starting to get involved more playing without the ball—screening shots for my teammates, cutting into and out of lanes, making myself a threat without the ball."

Even without the ball, Van Lier gets involved some way. He has too much competitive spark to only watch what's going on around him.

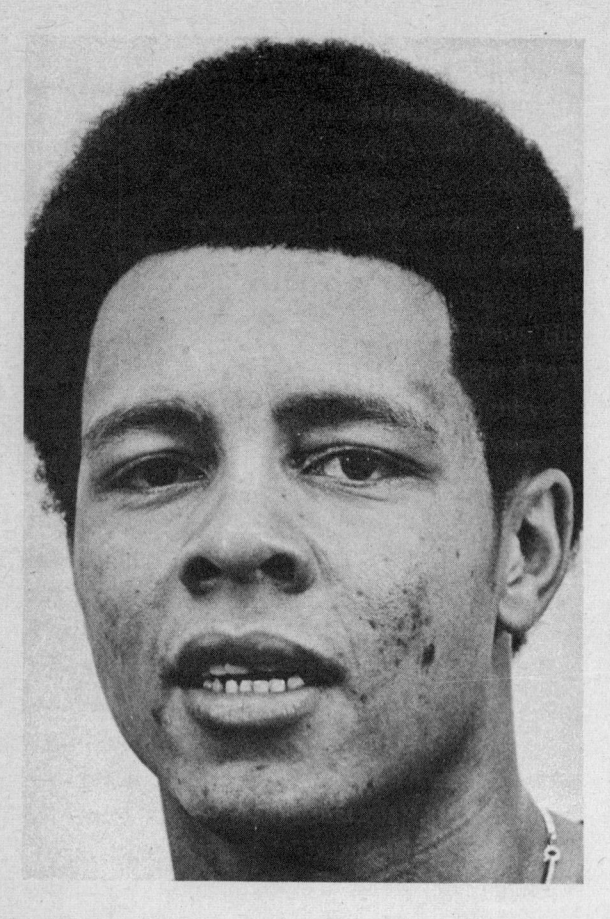

**Mack Calvin: ABA star sets sight on NBA stardom now.**

# MACK CALVIN
# Up From the ABA

The past couple of years, Mack Calvin made it a point to read the NBA box scores every day. It was a strange sight every morning. Calvin, who had played in the ABA for seven years, was studying who was scoring in the other league while he was having breakfast.

All those years Calvin knew he could play in the NBA. He was considered one of the best guards in the ABA, yet he never got recognition for his talents. The guards in the NBA got that. So Calvin just hoped and waited for his chance to play in the NBA.

He got it. When the ABA folded after the 1975-76 season, Calvin signed with the Los Angeles Lakers, the club that had originally drafted him on the 14th round in 1969.

"Mack Calvin will be a valuable asset to the Lakers," said Los Angeles general manager Pete Newell. "In addition to his quickness and shooting ability, he possesses a leadership quality that is always needed."

Calvin is typical of the small man with the big and varied talents. He is adept at taking the outlet pass from a center or forward who has snared a rebound and has passed off to Calvin to start the fast break. Calvin is equally able to either drive the entire length of the floor or hit the open man. He has the hands, the reflexes, and the eyes for the job and keeps his defensive foe guessing.

"It's when I'm doing things like that," he says, "that I'm glad I'm one of the little guys and not 6-8. For me, the fun comes in doing so many things."

Things like bringing the ball down and setting up the play.... Using his instinct to know when to penetrate or drive the baseline, or pass off to a forward.... Setting a slick screen for a teammate to shoot over.... Making a behind-the-back pass to a teammate cutting for the basket.... Releasing a jump shot so quickly that there's no chance of his opposing guard blocking the ball back in his face.

Mack Calvin is so quick he can shoot from outside or in close. He's also tough and isn't afraid to drive in for a lay-up with enemy arms and shoulders slashing away at him.

"Being small, I have learned to be tough," said Calvin. "I realize that I can't get all my points from outside, that I have to drive toward the basket. But that's what a guard has to do, be able to drive.

"Naturally, the baskets don't come easy. I have to fight for them by out-muscling my opponent. I first try to get position on him and then use my elbows inside when the going gets rough. That's the only way to get your opponent to respect you, by taking charge."

Calvin also feels there is another benefit a little man can gain in driving for the basket, and that is drawing fouls. Calvin draws a lot of them and says he gets as much satisfaction sinking foul shots as he does field goals. The fact is Calvin has scored more foul shots than field goals and is extremely accurate from the foul line with a remarkable career average of 87 percent.

"Shooting fouls is often an overlooked part of the little guy's game," said Calvin. "I spend a lot of time practicing foul shots. It requires a great amount of concentration. But it pays off. During a game, those one-point shots add up.

"A guard has to do it all and I work on all parts of my game, especially passing. Being a top passer can account for a lot of baskets."

But Calvin has another thing going for him that other NBA guards are not aware of. When he played in the ABA, Calvin kept a notebook containing notes on every guard he played against.

"It gives me an edge on defense," said Calvin. "I feel it's a smart thing to do. Before a game starts I know just what to expect from my opponent and I am able to anticipate some of his moves before he makes them."

He has a new notebook now for his new NBA foes.

During the past seven years, Calvin's quickness, shooting, and playmaking made him one of the top guards in the ABA. In his last season with the Squires, he averaged 19.3 points and six assists a game. His career averages of 20.1 points and 5.7 assists rank as some of the best in the ABA. In five of the last six years, the 27-year-old Calvin was selected to the ABA All-Star team and in 1975 he was named All-League.

Actually, Calvin is returning home. Born in Fort Worth, Texas, Calvin's family moved to Los Angeles when he was only six years old. It wasn't an easy move. Being the new kid on the block had its drawbacks.

"As far back as I can remember, I was the smallest kid in my class," Calvin recalls. "The others always pushed me around and wouldn't let me play. I lived in a tough neighborhood, and I had to learn to fight back."

So while Calvin learned to be tough, others learned that he was also quick. He wasn't so easy to push around. Although he was short as far as height went, he wasn't lacking in quickness and natural ability. And while his quickness got him through grade school, his athletic ability made it easier for him in high school.

At Long Beach Poly, Calvin developed into a shortstop who was good enough to be drafted by the Los Angeles Dodgers. Which was flattery enough. But between his junior and senior years, a big change took place with Calvin. He grew from 5-6 to 5-10, became infatuated with basketball, and practically forgot about baseball. Calvin worked hard at basketball, constantly seeking to improve.

"I had been the third guard on our state championship team when I was a junior," recalls Calvin. "But I wanted to play more and become a member of the starting team. I was determined to do it. That summer, prior to my senior year, I played basketball nine or 10 hours a day. I wouldn't quit. When there wasn't anybody around to play with, I practiced by myself, dribbling, shooting, jumping. I came home tired, but I came home realizing I gave it all I had."

It paid off, too. In his final year in high school, Calvin was a starting guard. He averaged 17 points a game and made All-League and All-State honorable mention. He helped to lead Long Beach Poly to another championship.

Calvin anxiously looked forward to college. But the college scouts overlooked him. Instead, they were more impressed with three of Calvin's teammates who were much taller. They received scholarships, while Calvin managed to get a two-year grant to Long Beach City College.

"The bigger colleges never approached me," recalled Calvin. "They didn't even know who I was. I guess they wrote me off as being too small for big-time college basketball."

After playing his two years at Long Beach, the big-college recruiters finally noticed him. By now they couldn't miss him. He helped spark Long Beach to a 65-3 record. It was no wonder that 40 colleges approached him for his final two years of college basketball. He had some attractive offers, namely one from UCLA, who had one of its usual powerhouses, featuring Lew Alcindor (Kareem Abdul-Jabbar).

However, Calvin decided to attend crosstown rival USC. He figured his chances of playing there were better. Calvin established himself as a starter at USC and helped to hand UCLA one of its two losses during its Lew Alcindor years. Quite naturally, Calvin looked forward to playing professional basketball.

But despite the fact that he grew to a half inch over six feet, the pros felt Calvin wasn't big enough. Although he was a hometown product, the NBA Lakers picked him on the 14th round and the player-hungry ABA Stars waited until the seventh round to select him.

"The Lakers picking me so low meant only one

Calvin, as Virginia Squire, battles for a loose ball.

thing," reasoned Calvin. "It meant I could probably go to their tryout camp, pick up a free Coke, and go home. I figured I had a better shot with the Stars."

He was right. Calvin not only made the ABA team, but he broke into the starting lineup, which isn't an easy accomplishment for a rookie. He averaged almost 17 points a game and was named to the league's All-Rookie team. He was off to a great start and Sharman was showing him how.

After an excellent beginning, frustration took over. It began when Calvin was traded to the newly formed Miami Floridians shortly after his fine rookie season. Calvin felt really low.

"I was surprised and hurt," admitted Calvin. "It meant that I would have to leave home for the first time. I was so shook up I cried."

Calvin didn't know what to expect with a new team and a new coach when he reported to the Floridians. But when coach Hal Blitman observed Calvin in training camp, he knew immediately what to do. He decided to build a guard-orientated offense around him and Larry Jones.

The determined Calvin more than responded to the challenge. He averaged 27.2 points a game, which was fourth best in the ABA. Even though he was named to the All-League team, he didn't get the full recognition he deserved. He was looked upon strictly as a scorer. Still, his fine season helped to make up for some of the frustration of leaving home and playing with a new team.

But the following season, the frustration returned. The financially troubled Floridians were disbanded after the 1971-72 season. He was placed in a player pool and was selected by the Carolina Cougars. It meant that Calvin would be playing with his third team in four years. It wasn't exactly the way he thought pro ball would be.

But under coach Larry Brown, and along with star forwards Billy Cunningham and Joe Caldwell, Calvin developed into a complete player. The newly found success pleased him.

"Offensively," he says, "I tried to be a playmaker as well as a scorer. I'll only take the shot if the defense gives it to me. What I concentrated on was dividing the offense between Cunningham and Caldwell up front. If the defense took that away, then it left me or somebody else open for the shot. Our attack depended upon the involvement of the whole team. It helped me a great deal in not having to carry the whole load.

"Defensively, our style was suited to me. I was allowed to gamble more in going for the pass. I pressed more and at times overplayed my opponent, which worked fine because of my quickness in being able to recover. What made it all so pleasing was the fact that we were winning. I couldn't have asked for a better situation."

But the situation didn't last. Before the 1974-75 season, Calvin was traded to the Denver Nuggets. Once again, a feeling of failure began to settle in. But Calvin learned to adjust. He took some karate lessons and later visited a hypnotist to help him overcome his moving around and a fear of flying.

"Karate helped my physical strength, quickness, and overall confidence," claimed Calvin. "It's a form of meditation. It also helped me gain more poise and self-discipline."

But Calvin also managed to learn a few more tricks on the basketball court, even while being traded from Denver to the ill-fated Virginia Squires after the 1974-75 season. That made his fifth ABA team in seven years. He couldn't have traveled much more if he played for the Harlem Globetrotters.

"I'm picking up the pro tricks—an elbow in a bigger guy's belly and all that," confided Calvin. "I have to do these things to make up for my height. I've also filled out a bit more and this helps. I'm not getting pushed around like I did at the beginning."

He also hopes he won't have to move around any more. When he signed with the Lakers, it marked his sixth club in eight years of pro basketball. But at least Los Angeles is home. And Calvin never wanted to leave home to begin with.